SCIENCE
MAKERS

Making with
LIVING
THINGS

Anna Claybourne

BUILD AMAZING PROJECTS WITH INSPIRATIONAL SCIENTISTS, ARTISTS AND ENGINEERS

Published in paperback in Great Britain in 2020 by Wayland
Copyright © Hodder and Stoughton, 2018

Editor: Sarah Silver
Designer: Eoin Norton
Picture researcher: Diana Morris

ISBN 978 1 5263 0545 9

All photographs by Eoin Norton for Wayland except the following:
Stefano Bianchetti/Corbis via Getty Images: 14tr. A. Barrington Brown/SPL: 26tl.
Steve Crukov/Shutterstock: 21cr. Photo courtesy of the French Ministry of Culture and
Communication, Rhône-Alpes region: 5b. © Antony Gormley. Figure, Another Place 2005/
photo Sallycinnamon/Getty Images: 22cr. Big Jamnong/Shutterstock: 10tr. Victoria Ki/
Shutterstock: 13bl. Kletr/Shutterstock: 15bl. Rene-Theophile-Hyacinthe_Laennec/CC
Wikimedia Commons: 20cl, 20cr. LOC: 16tl. Lyme Regis Museum/CC Wikimedia Commons:
28cl. Richard A McMillin/Shutterstock: 5t. David McNew/Getty Images: 29cr. Oleksandr
Meinyk/Dreamstime: 20tl. MriMAn/Shutterstock: 4b. Naddya/Shutterstock: 18tl.
Nejron Photo/Shutterstock: 25br. © Numen/For Use. Photographer Aurélie Cenno: 18c,
18cb. Annie Owen/RobertHarding/Superstock: 10tl. NicholaS Piccillo/Shutterstock:
9bl. PD/Wikimedia Commons: 28tr. Sabphoto/Shutterstock: 17br. Johannes Simon/
AFP/Getty Images: 22tl. Ullsteinbild/Getty Images: 14tl. CC Wikimedia Commons: 6tl,
6tc, 8t, 16tr. Attapol Yiemsiriwut/Shutterstock: 13br. Dora Zett/Shutterstock: 5c.

FSC
www.fsc.org

MIX
Paper from
responsible sources
FSC® C104740

Printed in Dubai

Wayland, an imprint of
Hachette Children's Group
Part of Hodder and Stoughton
Carmelite House
50 Victoria Embankment
London EC4Y 0DZ

An Hachette UK Company
www.hachette.co.uk
www.hachettechildrens.co.uk

Note:
In preparation of this book, all due care has been exercised with regard to the instructions,
activities and techniques depicted. The publishers regret that they can accept no liability for any
loss or injury sustained. Always follow manufacturers' advice when handling plaster of Paris.

The website addresses (URLs) included in this book were valid at the time of going to press.
However, because of the nature of the Internet, it is possible that some addresses may have
changed, or sites may have changed or closed down since publication. While the author
and publishers regret any inconvenience this may cause to the readers, no responsibility
for any such changes can be accepted by either the author or the publishers.

CONTENTS

TAKE CARE!

These projects can be made with everyday objects, materials and tools that you can find at home, or in a supermarket, hobby store or DIY store. However, some do involve working with things that are sharp or breakable, or need extra strength to operate. Make sure you have an adult on hand to supervise and to help with anything that could be dangerous, and get permission before you try out any of the projects.

UNDERSTANDING LIVING THINGS

We are used to seeing life all around us. We humans are living things ourselves, and so are grass, trees and other plants, our pets, wild animals, fungi, and the bacteria that cause diseases. In fact, there are millions of different species (types) of living things on our planet – and life has existed here for billions of years.

We don't know exactly how or where life first began. However, scientists have found that all living things are related. They all use the chemical DNA, found inside cells, as a way of storing and passing on information that controls how each species grows and survives.

All the world's living things developed from the first life forms, and are related to each other in a huge family tree.

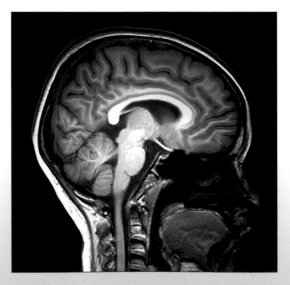

The human brain is one of the most complex objects ever known.

WHAT IS LIFE?

There are several things that all living things do, which help us to define exactly what is life, and what is not life. For example, living things take in food, grow, sense their surroundings, and make copies of themselves, or have babies. Living things are complex, and some, like humans, are also intelligent and creative.

THE SCIENCE OF LIFE

The study of living things, known as biology, is one of the most important aspects of science. It means studying ourselves, and the plants, animals and ecosystems that we depend on for food. Studying life and how living things work has allowed humans to come up with all kinds of incredibly useful inventions, such as farming and breeding animals, using plants to make cotton fabric, and making medicines to treat illnesses.

We use the fluffy seed coverings of the cotton plant to make fabric for clothes.

Humans have created many different dog breeds by breeding from a wild animal, the grey wolf.

LIVING THINGS AND ART

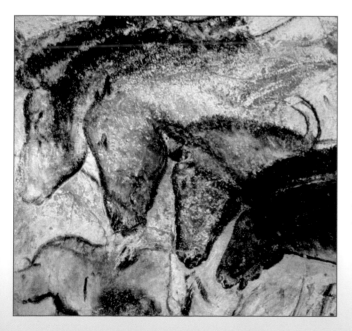

Living things have inspired artists since ancient times. Most of the earliest known artworks are models or cave paintings of animals. Paintings and sculptures ever since have featured flowers, trees and forests, animals and our own human bodies and faces. Some artists have used living things to control or create artworks themselves. Some are inspired by the way living things grow and change, to make artworks that do the same. Others use film and photography to try to capture the essence of life.

An amazingly lifelike, 17,000-year-old cave drawing of horses, found in Lascaux, France.

MINIATURE PLANT WORLD

Make your own terrarium, a type of tiny greenhouse accidentally invented by Nathaniel Bagshaw Ward.

MAKER PROFILE:

Nathaniel Bagshaw Ward
(1791–1868)

Nathaniel Bagshaw Ward was a doctor in London, but in his spare time he studied plants and insects. In one experiment in 1829, Ward put a moth pupa into some soil inside a jar, and screwed the lid on. A few days later he noticed plants growing in the soil. Ward realised that water was evaporating, then condensing and running down the sides of the jar – so the soil always stayed damp, and plants could live inside. Based on this, he invented a mini-greenhouse, the Wardian case, now known as a terrarium.

Victorian explorers used Wardian cases to transport tropical plants back to Britain on long sea journeys.

WHAT YOU NEED

- a large, clear glass or plastic jar with a lid
- gravel or small stones
- activated charcoal (from a garden centre or pet shop)
- potting compost
- a jug of water
- a fork
- a spray bottle
- a small plant (or several if your jar is large enough), such as miniature violets, begonias, ferns and club moss

1.

Step 1.
Wash and dry your jar and lid. Add a layer of stones or gravel about 1–2 cm deep, then a layer of activated charcoal about 1–2 cm deep. Spread them out gently with the fork.

2.

Step 2.
Now add a layer of potting compost about 3-6 cm deep. Use the fork to level and pat down the compost, and to dig a hole for the plant to fit into.

3.

Step 3.
Water your plant well, leaving it to soak for a few minutes. Then remove it from its pot and plant it in the soil. Press down the compost around the plant with the fork.

4.

Step 4.
Fill the spray bottle with water and spray the plant, the compost and the sides of the jar with water several times each.

5.

Step 5.
Put the lid on and leave the terrarium somewhere safe, where it will receive daylight, but not direct bright sunlight (which could overheat it). Check it each day, and add a little more water if it looks dry.

ROUND AND ROUND

As Ward realised, a Wardian case or terrarium is like a mini ecosystem or mini planet Earth, with its own water cycle. The water evaporates into the air, then rises and reaches the top, where it cools, condenses, and 'rains' back down into the soil. As it moves around in the cycle, it passes through the soil, plants and trees, helping them to grow.

Plants also need the gas carbon dioxide. They take it from the air and give out oxygen. Meanwhile, bacteria in the soil give out carbon dioxide and take in oxygen, helping to keep the plants alive. Opening the terrarium once every few days will also help to refresh the air inside.

FAST FLOWERS

Copy John Ott and make an amazing speeded-up film of a flower opening.

MAKER PROFILE:

John Ott
(1909–2000)

John Ott was an American photographer who made early time-lapse films. He was fascinated by the idea of capturing slow changes, such as a flower opening, on film, so that they could be watched speeded up. His photography started as a hobby, but soon took over his life as he designed and built more and more camera contraptions and devices to photograph his greenhouses full of plants. He became famous for his work, which was used in several films, and also wrote books about his methods.

WHAT YOU NEED

- fresh cut flower buds, such as irises, daffodils or tulips
- scissors
- a glass or small vase
- warm water
- a smartphone with a time-lapse function (see panel below)
- a tripod, or some books and sticky tack

If your phone doesn't have a time-lapse function, you can use a time-lapse app, such as OSnap! or Hyperlapse. Choose one that will work with your phone, and follow the instructions to set it up to make a time-lapse film over several hours.

1.

2.

Step 1.

For your film, choose flower buds that are starting to open and have some colour showing. Cut off the bottoms of the stems at a sharp angle.

Step 2.

Fill the glass or vase with warm (not hot) tap water and stand the flowers in it. (This helps them to open faster.)

Step 3.

Put the glass or vase indoors in artificial light, so that the lighting won't change too much. Set up your time-lapse function or app ready to use, but don't start it yet.

Step 4.

Set up your phone on the tripod, pointing at the flowers. If you don't have a tripod, stand the phone up between two piles of books, with strips of sticky tack along the bottom to hold it in place.

3&4.

5.

6.

Step 5.

Keep checking the flowers, and wait until you see at least one of them just beginning to open. At this point, start the time-lapse film running.

Step 6.

Leave the phone filming for as long as possible, or until the flower has fully opened (it may take several hours). The film should be stored just like a normal video, which you can then save, view and share. Because it has far fewer frames than a normal video, it should not take up too much memory space.

FRAME BY FRAME

A normal film or video is made of lots of separate photographs, or frames, taken multiple times per second. For a time-lapse film, the camera shoots a frame much less often – for example, once every minute. Then it plays them back quickly, like a normal video. This reveals a speeded-up version of something that happens very slowly in real life. As well as looking fascinating, time-lapse photography can be very useful for scientists studying things like plants, insect life cycles and the growth of bacteria or algae.

NATURAL TIE-DYE

Dye fabric amazing colours and patterns, using non-toxic plant dyes from your fridge, cupboard or supermarket.

MAKER PROFILE:

Ancient Indian dyers
(From c. 2500 BCE)

The ancient people of what is now India were famous for their skills at colouring cloth with natural dyes. They used plants such as indigo, turmeric and madder, or animals such as the lac insect, and described them in ancient Indian writings, such as the Vedas. The Indian tradition of colourful dyeing has continued ever since, and some people still use the old traditional methods and plant dyes.

Natural products such as indigo for blue (above) and dried flowers for yellow (above right) are still used to create dyes today.

WHAT YOU NEED

- a piece of plain white or cream 100 per cent natural fabric, such as cotton or linen
- a large saucepan
- a cooking hob
- a measuring jug
- table salt
- an old wooden spoon
- old newspapers
- an old tea towel or pillowcase
- a vegetable knife
- strong, thin cotton string or extra-strength sewing thread
- scissors
- fruit, vegetables or spices to dye with (see box on page 11)

Your fabric has to be able to fit inside the pan, so make sure your piece isn't too big. Make it around the size of a tea towel, or smaller.

10

1 & 2.

3 & 4.

Step 1.
If your fabric is new, wash it in a washing machine before using it. This removes any chemicals or surface coatings that may have been added to it in the factory.

Step 2.
With an adult to help, fill the saucepan with hot tap water, and stir in some salt. There should be 1 part salt to 16 parts water. For example, if you have 1,600 ml of water, use 100 ml of salt.

Step 3.
Put the fabric into the salty water, and push it under with the spoon. Ask the adult to heat the pan up until the water boils, and simmer the fabric for an hour, stirring occasionally. This helps the fabric to soak up the dye more easily.

Step 4.
After an hour, ask the adult to pour away the hot water, leave the fabric to cool, then wring it out. Ask the adult to refill the pan with hot water and heat it up again until it boils.

5.

Here are some of the plant dyes you could use, and the colours you might get from them:

Beetroot – pinkish-purple
Blueberries – blueish-purple
Red cabbage – blueish-purple
Brown onion skins – orangey yellow
Red onion skins – pink
Teabags – light brown
Turmeric powder – yellow
Spinach – green
Bay leaves – yellow
Blackberries – purple
Cherries – pink

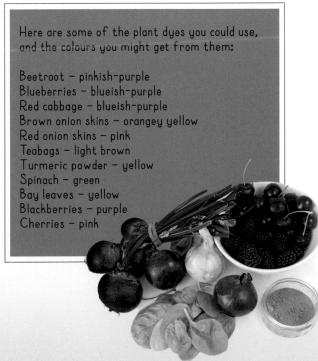

Step 5
With adult help, add a plant dye, such as turmeric powder or crushed berries, to the water, and let it simmer. For one pan of water, use a large handful of fruit or vegetables, or one pack of turmeric. If you're using beetroot, ask an adult to chop it into small pieces.

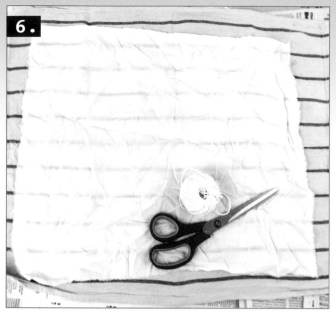

Step 6.

Spread newspaper on the floor, somewhere away from carpets, such as in the kitchen or bathroom. Lie an old tea towel or pillowcase on the newspaper, and spread out your damp fabric on top.

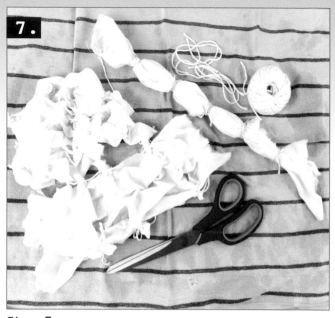

Step 7.

Cut pieces of string around 15–30 cm long, and tie them around the fabric in different patterns. For example, you could pinch or twist small pieces of the fabric and wrap thread tightly around them. Or fold or crumple the whole piece of fabric and tie string tightly around it in sections.

Step 8.

When your fabric is all tied up, ask an adult to lower it gently into the hot dye bath, or pan of dye, and push it under with the wooden spoon. They should keep stirring it and turning it over every few minutes.

Step 9

Simmer the fabric for at least another hour, then turn the heat off and leave the fabric in the pan until it has completely cooled down. Ask an adult to pour away the water and throw away any bits of plant material.

10.

Step 10.
Rinse your fabric bundle in water. Carefully, without cutting into the fabric, snip off the pieces of string or thread. Spread out the fabric and rinse it again, then wring it out and hang it up to dry.

Fabric dyed this way will not be completely colourfast, as this requires stronger chemicals – so avoid washing it in the washing machine. But you can use it to make things like bunting, a cushion cover, or a decoration for a bag.

PLANT PIGMENTS

Fruit, vegetables, flowers and plants are mostly very colourful – but why? Plants contain pigments, or coloured chemicals, for lots of reasons. Plants use the green chemical chlorophyll, found in leaves, to harvest energy from sunlight. Berries are often a bright colour, like red or yellow, to help them stand out. This makes it easier for birds to see and eat them, and spread the plants' seeds around in their dropping. Purplish pigments called anthocyanins are thought to help plants recover from damage. Chopping, crushing and heating plant material helps to break down the plant cells and release the pigments. They can then soak into the fibres of a natural fabric such as cotton.

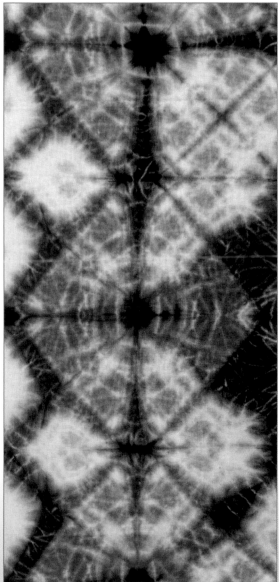

CLOSE-UP
CREEPY CRAWLIES

We often ignore or even run away from creepy-crawlies. Instead, make a bug viewer and take a closer look!

MAKER PROFILE:

Jean-Henri Fabre
(1823–1915)

By the time he died aged 91, Jean-Henri Fabre was renowned as a great entomologist, or insect scientist. Yet he was mostly self-taught, studying insects as a hobby while working as a teacher. For many years he was not taken seriously. At the time, most naturalists simply caught and killed insects and examined their bodies. Fabre preferred to work with living creatures, watching their behaviour and how they survived. To help him do this, he used all kinds of everyday objects, like sieves, bowls, jars and bottles, to help him capture and inspect his insects safely.

Some of Fabre's equipment at his home, now a museum, in Provence, France.

You rip up the animal and I study it alive; you turn it into an object of horror and pity, whereas I cause it to be loved.
– Jean-Henri Fabre

WHAT YOU NEED

- a clear or translucent plastic container with a thin, flexible plastic lid
- a plastic magnifying lens or plastic magnifying glass, smaller than the lid
- a marker pen
- scissors or craft knife
- a strong glue or hot glue gun
- a large needle

1.

2.

3.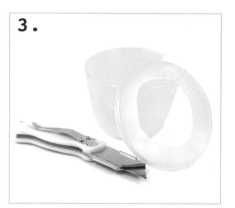

4.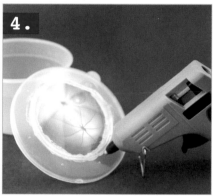

5.

6.

Step 1.
If you have a magnifying glass with a handle, ask an adult to remove the lens from the frame, or remove the handle, if possible. (If not, you can leave it on.)

Step 2.
Place the magnifying glass lens on the middle of the container lid, and draw around it with the marker.

Step 3.
Ask an adult to cut about 0.5 cm inside the line using scissors or a craft knife, to make a hole that is smaller than the lens.

Step 4.
Ask an adult to use strong glue or a hot glue gun to put glue all around the edge of the hole. Stick the lens over the hole, making sure there are no gaps, and leave to dry.

Step 5.
Use the needle to make a ring of small air holes around the edge of the lid.

Step 6.
When you find a creepy-crawly to view, take the lid off the viewer, and gently brush the insect into the container, or push it in with a piece of card. Press the lid back on and look through the lens. When you've had a good look, let your creepy-crawly go.

IN CLOSE-UP

Creepy-crawlies are fascinating and amazing to look at, but it can be hard to see all the details because they're often so small. A lens has a curved surface that bends the light that comes from objects towards our eyes. The bent rays of light make the object appear to be much bigger than it is.

ANIMAL FLICK BOOK

How do horses run? Eadweard Muybridge wanted to find out, so he invented a way of capturing every step – and found a way of animating images in the process.

MAKER PROFILE:

Eadweard Muybridge
(1830–1904)

Eadweard Muybridge was one of the first British photographers. In 1872, racehorse owner Leland Stanford asked Muybridge to use photography to find out whether horses completely left the ground as they ran (a popular debate at the time). Muybridge set up a row of cameras, each one triggered by a string stretched across a track. As a horse ran along it, the cameras photographed every stage of its movement. Muybridge also invented a device called the zoopraxiscope. It displayed the photographs quickly in sequence, creating a moving image.

Muybridge's zoopraxiscope, along with a glass picture disk used to make a moving image.

Only photography has been able to divide human life into a series of moments. Each of them has the value of a complete existence.
- Eadweard Muybridge

WHAT YOU NEED

- a computer, printer and paper
- scissors
- a small, thick notebook
- paper glue

1.

Step 1.
Find a good, clear image of *The Horse in Motion*, or another of Muybridge's animal movement sequences, on the Internet. Print it out, making the image as big as possible on the printer paper. One copy will work, but to make a longer flick book, you could print out extra copies.

2.

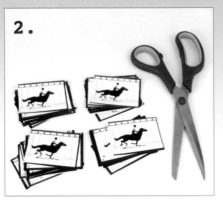

Step 2.
Cut the printouts up neatly into their individual frames, making sure you keep them all in the right order! If you have more than one printout, make each page into a separate pile of cut-out pictures.

3.

Step 3.
Take the first photograph and glue it into the first page of your notebook. Line it up with the outside edge of the page. Use only a small amount of glue to avoid weighing the page down.

4.

Step 4.
Stick the next picture in the exact same place on the next page. Continue glueing the pictures, in sequence, on to the pages. When you finish the first pile, move on to the next, until they are all used up or you run out of pages.

PUTTING IT TOGETHER

Film, video and animated cartoons work by showing the viewer a series of still images in quick succession. Muybridge's zoopraxiscope did this too, and so does a flick book. This is different from real life, where things really do move continuously. Yet the viewer still sees the image 'moving' in a realistic way.

It works because if the brain receives images of something in two different positions close together, it automatically 'fills in' movement between them – making human and animal movements look lifelike and realistic on the screen. Scientists aren't sure how it works – but the whole film and TV industry relies on it!

5.

Step 5.
Separate all the pages from each other in case any have stuck together. Leave the glue to dry completely. Then hold the book in your left hand, and flick through the pages with your right, to see the animal moving.

Most movie projectors move the film at a speed of 24 frames per second.

WEAVE A WEB

Copy spiders and learn how to spin your own web, like art collective Numen/For Use.

MAKER PROFILE:

Numen/For Use
(Founded in 1999)

Numen/For Use is the name of a European art collective, or team, with three members: Sven Jonke, Christoph Katzler and Nikola Radeljković. They are industrial designers who also work together to make large-scale art installations, often inspired by natural processes and living systems. Among other artworks, they have created several huge webs, made from tape or string and suspended across whole gallery spaces, courtyards, rivers or parks, as if left there by enormous spiders.

The Numen art collective (l-r: Christoph Katzler, Sven Jonke and Nikola Radeljković), inside one of their giant webs.

Tape Hasselt, House for Contemporary Art, Hasselt, Belgium, 2012.

WHAT YOU NEED

- a large ball of string or knitting yarn
- scissors
- nails or screw-in hooks
- a hammer
- a place to attach your web to — it could be in the corner of a room indoors, or between trees or fences outdoors

The first architecture ever made, by animals, is made the same way, like this.
– *Sven Jonke*

Step 1.
Decide where you are going to put your web. You will need three or four anchor points to tie the string to.

Step 2.
Ask an adult to put nails or hooks into the walls or door frames to make the anchor points. (Make sure whoever owns the building is OK with this first!) If you're outdoors, you could tie the string or yarn around fenceposts and tree branches instead.

Step 3.
Unroll your string or yarn and tie the end firmly to one of your fixing points. Stretch it tightly to the next point, and tie or attach it there. Tie the string or yarn to your next chosen anchor point, and continue, until finally bringing it back to back to the point you started at. Tie the string there again, and snip off the rest.

Step 4.
You should now have a large square, rectangle or triangle shape. Cut lengths of string or yarn and tie them across the shape, from one side to the other, so that they all cross each other in the middle, and snip off the loose ends.

Step 5.
Tie a long piece of string or yarn to the middle of the web, and start spiralling it around and around, working outwards. Each time you come to one of the strings, tie the thread around it. If you use up your string, tie another piece to it.

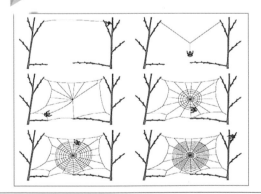

Step 6.
When you reach the outer edge, knot the string or yarn, and snip the rest off.

SPIDER SCIENCE

The steps for building this spiral web are the same ones that real spiders use. Spiders make webs to catch their prey, but unlike us, they don't have to learn how. Web-spinning behaviour is an instinct — an automatic behaviour that the spider does naturally.

A web like this makes a great bedroom feature or party decoration. You could even make a rainbow web using a combination of different colours. Or try clingfilm twisted into a thin rope — it makes a semi-transparent, slightly sticky web.

HEAR YOUR HEART

The stethoscope is a brilliantly simple listening device that helps doctors hear what's going on inside the human body. Once you've made one, try some tests on your heart.

MAKER PROFILE:

René Laennec
(1781–1826)

In 1816, René Laennec was a busy doctor in a large hospital in Paris. One day, he was having problems checking a patient's heartbeat. He remembered that he'd recently seen children playing with wooden tubes, making noises at one end and listening at the other. So he rolled several sheets of paper into a tube, held one end to the woman's heart, and put his ear to the other. It worked! He heard the patient's heartbeat loud and clear. Following this discovery Laennec designed a simple hollow wooden tube with a listening piece at one end. He had invented the first version of the stethoscope – which gets its name from the Greek words for 'chest-looking'.

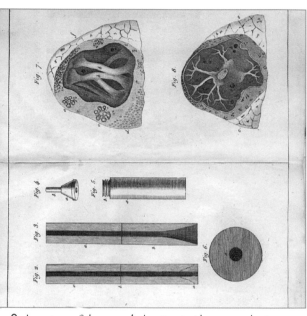

A drawing of Laennec's basic stethoscope design.

WHAT YOU NEED

- about 45 cm of flexible plastic tubing from a hardware or DIY store
- two small funnels
- sticky tape
- a watch or timer
- pen and paper

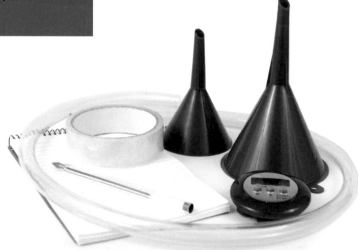

I immediately saw that this might become an indispensable method for studying, not only the beating of the heart, but all movements able of producing sound in the chest cavity.
– René Laennec

20

1.

2.

Step 1.

Connect one end of the tubing to one of the funnels. If one doesn't fit inside the other, line them up and join them with sticky tape. Do the same with the other funnel at the other end.

Step 2.

Hold one funnel to your ear, and press the other against your chest, just left of the middle. You should be able to hear your heart beating.

3.

Step 3.

To test your heart, sit still for a few minutes, then listen to your heartbeat. Use the watch or timer to count how many times your heart beats in 15 seconds.

INTO YOUR EARS

Like other tube-shaped sound inventions, the stethoscope carries and directs sound waves. Instead of spreading out in all directions and becoming much quieter, the sounds of the heart are channelled along the tube and into the ear. The stethoscope became even more effective when later inventors improved it, using flexible tubes that linked to both ears instead of one. Today, although it's not a hi-tech device, every doctor still has a stethoscope.

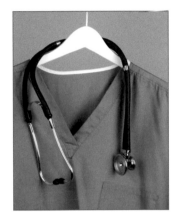

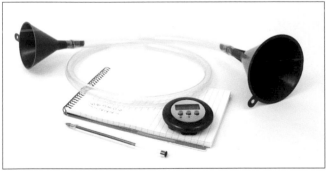

For example: 20 beats in 15 seconds.
Multiply this by 4 to give your heart rate per minute.
20 x 4 = 80 beats per minute.

As René Laennec realised, the stethoscope can be used to listen to other body parts too. You could use yours to try listening to your lungs, your stomach after a big meal, or your intestines.

Try measuring your heartbeat before and after doing star jumps for 30 seconds. Is it different?

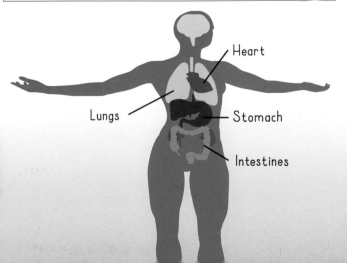

Heart

Lungs

Stomach

Intestines

BODY COPY

Create an artwork by making a cast of your own body. Instead of using your entire body, like maker Antony Gormley, start with just a hand – it's a bit easier!

MAKER PROFILE:

Antony Gormley
(1950–)

Sir Antony Gormley is a leading British sculptor who is best-known for using casts of his own body to make many of his works. As well as appearing in galleries, the body-shaped sculptures have been installed in city streets, on top of buildings, on a beach and in many other locations.

Gormley makes the casts by covering his body in clingfilm to protect his skin, then he is coated in plaster by two assistants. This makes a mould which can then be used to cast the sculpture. Gormley often adds other parts and shapes to the figures too, such as ridges or wings, or a surface texture.

One of the body cast figures from Antony Gormley's work *Another Place*.

All the proportions that mean things to us as human beings are related to the body.
– Antony Gormley

WHAT YOU NEED

- old newspapers
- a large, empty plastic drinks bottle
- a ruler
- a marker pen
- strong scissors
- petroleum jelly or baby oil
- 500 g bag of alginate powder (see below)
- a mixing bowl or large plastic jug
- an electric hand-held mixer
- a measuring jug
- plaster of Paris
- a clean, empty large yoghurt pot or ice cream tub
- a lolly stick or craft stick
- measuring cups

Alginate is a non-toxic, jelly-like moulding material made from seaweed. It's easy to find in hobby stores or online. Any alginate that gets onto your hands, equipment or kitchen surfaces will peel off easily once it's dry.

1&2.

3.

Step 1.
Decide which hand you are going to make a cast of. Remove any jewellery or plasters and wash and dry your hand. Spread out newspapers to work on.

Step 2.
Measure 25 cm up from the base of your plastic bottle, and mark a line there. Use the scissors to cut off the top of the bottle (with an adult to help if necessary).

Step 3.
Check the instructions on your alginate to find out how much water to add, and measure out the amount in your measuring jug. Tip the alginate powder into the mixing bowl. Ask an adult to plug in the electric mixer and have it ready.

4.

5.

Step 4.
Rub a small amount of petroleum jelly or baby oil all over the hand you are going to cast, including a little way up the arm. Have the cut-off bottle ready too. You will need to do the next steps quite quickly, as the alginate sets in just a couple of minutes.

Step 5.
Pour the water into the alginate powder and ask the adult to mix it well with the electric mixer for about 20 seconds. Then they should quickly pour the mixture into the cut-off bottle, filling it about three-quarters full.

Step 6

Put your hand into the alginate mixture in the bottle, and push it down so that the mixture comes up over your wrist. Keep the hand still in the position you want, making sure it doesn't push against the sides of the bottle. Wait 2-3 minutes for the mixture to set.

Step 7.

Tap the top of the mixture to check it has set into a firm jelly. Then gently begin to wiggle your fingers and move your arm from side to side slightly, to let air into the space. Gradually and gently pull your hand out of the mould. As the alginate is flexible, this is not difficult.

WARNING

Always have an adult present when using plaster of Paris and do not pour unused plaster down the sink! It will set and block the pipes. Leave it to set in the tub, then throw the tub away.

Step 8.

Wash and dry your hand. Then measure out 1 cup of water into your yoghurt or ice cream tub, and add 1.5 cups of plaster of Paris powder. Stir with the lolly stick until the mixture is smooth and creamy.

Step 9.

Pour a little plaster of Paris into the alginate mould, so that it runs into the fingers and thumb, and tip the mould to and fro to help the plaster coat the inside. Then fill the mould with plaster up to the top of the alginate, and add a little more plaster to make a base.

Step 10.

Leave the plaster to harden for several hours. Then you can carefully cut down the side of the bottle and remove the plastic.

11.

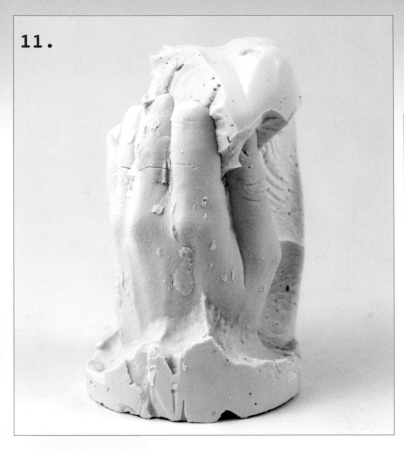

Step 11.
Carefully peel and cut the rubbery alginate away from the plaster. Inside you will find a plaster cast of your hand.

If the cast breaks or any fingers fall off, don't worry. Leave the parts a few more hours to dry out, then ask an adult to glue them back together with strong glue.

PERFECT COPIES

Casting is an ancient technique that has been used for thousands of years. By coating or covering an object with something soft that then sets, you can make a copy of it that picks up every tiny detail. Alginate is especially good for this. If you look at your hand cast, you should be able to see tiny wrinkles, and the texture of your skin.

For this reason, dentists use alginate to make casts of the inside of people's mouths. It's also used by special effects artists to make masks that will fit perfectly on to an actor's face.

You could use your hand cast as a sculpture, a ring holder, or a scary decoration. Once it's dry, it can be painted with acrylic or water-based paints. You can also make casts of your feet, in the same way, using a wider container.

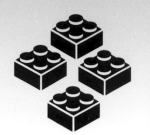

BUILDING BLOCKS OF LIFE

Make your own model of DNA, the molecule inside our cells that controls how living things grow and work.

MAKER PROFILE:

James Watson
(left) (1928–)
Francis Crick
(right) (1916–2004)

Today, we know a lot about genes, and DNA, the chemical they are made from. But it took many years and many scientists to discover DNA and how it worked. In 1953, British biologist Francis Crick and his American colleague James Watson managed to figure out a key part of the puzzle – the shape of the DNA molecule. To help them, they built a model of it, showing its spiral-ladder-like shape, known as a double helix.

WHAT YOU NEED

- a long wooden skewer
- strong garden wire
- wire cutters
- a block of polystyrene or slab of plasticine, to use as a base
- small polystyrene balls (from a hobby store)
- large wooden or plastic beads with large holes, all the same colour
- several pipe cleaners, all the same colour
- drinking straws in four different colours
- scissors

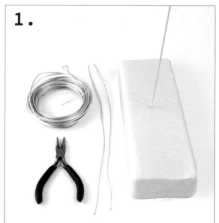

1.

Step 1.
Stick the skewer into the polystyrene or plasticine. Use the wire cutters to cut two lengths of wire, each about 50 per cent longer than the skewer.

2.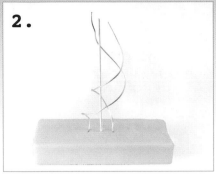

Step 2.
Gently bend the pieces of wire into spiral-shaped curves. Push the wires into the base, one on either side of the skewer, about 3 cm away from it, so that they spiral around it.

3.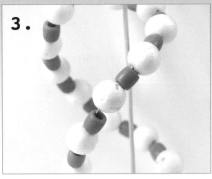

Step 3.
Now thread the polystyrene balls and beads onto the wires, in an alternating pattern. On each wire, put a ball, then a bead, then a ball, and so on, until they are fully covered.

4.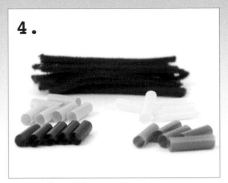

Step 4.
Cut the pipe cleaners into short sections about 8 cm long. Cut the straws into sections about 2 cm long. Arrange the straw pieces into two groups, each containing two colours.

5&6.

Step 5.
Take a piece of pipe cleaner and thread two different-coloured pieces of straw onto it from one of the piles. Push one end of the pipe cleaner into one of the polystyrene balls at the bottom of the model.

Step 6.
Wrap the pipe cleaner around the wooden skewer between the two pieces of straw. Push the other end of the pipe cleaner into the polystyrene ball on the other side.

7.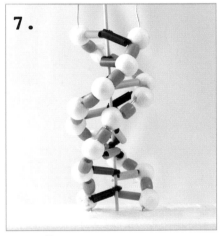

Step 7.
Continue adding 'rungs' of the ladder in the same way until you reach the top, always pairing the same sets of two colours together, alternating the pairs each time.

DNA

The shape and structure of DNA is very important. The two sides of the 'ladder' can separate, and collect new parts to make two new matching copies of the DNA. This is how DNA is copied when cells divide, and when new cells, seeds or babies are made.

Adenine, cytosine, guanine and thymine are four chemicals known as bases, which make up part of the structure of DNA.

STRUCTURE OF DNA

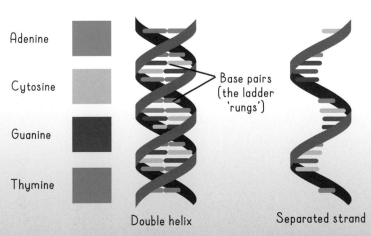

Adenine

Cytosine

Guanine

Thymine

Base pairs (the ladder 'rungs')

Double helix

Separated strand

FABULOUS FOSSILS

Make a realistic-looking fake fossil, or even create your own imaginary fossil creature.

MAKER PROFILE:

Mary Anning
(1799–1847)

Mary Anning was a British fossil collector and palaeontologist (fossil scientist). Near her home in Lyme Regis, England, she discovered important ichthyosaur, plesiosaur and pterosaur fossils. Anning was also a skilled artist, making detailed drawings of her finds in order to share information about them with other fossil experts. Palaeontologists of the time also made plaster casts of fossils, so that they could transport, display and study the copies without damaging the original.

A cast of the skull of one of the ichthyosaurs (sea reptiles) Anning discovered.

WHAT YOU NEED

- items to cast, such as small fossils, seashells, bones or teeth
- old newspapers
- lots of plasticine
- a flattish stone, smaller then the plasticine
- petroleum jelly or baby oil
- plaster of Paris
- measuring cups
- a clean, empty large yoghurt pot or ice cream tub
- a lolly stick or a craft stick
- paints (optional)

1.

Step 1.

Shape your plasticine into a slab about 3-4 cm thick. Make sure your stone is clean, then rub it with petroleum jelly or baby oil. Press it firmly into the plasticine, then carefully lift it out.

Step 2.

Take the item you want to cast, such as a shell. Press it into the middle of the indentation made by the stone, then pull it out. It will leave a copy of its shape behind. You can make several different moulds, if you have enough plasticine.

2.

FOSSIL FORMATION

Fossils themselves are a kind of cast. They can form when objects like bones or shells are trapped under layers of sand or mud that slowly harden into rock. The bone or shell eventually dissolves away, leaving a space in the rock that is filled with stony minerals.

3.

Step 3.

Spread out newspapers to work on. Measure one cupful of water and pour it into the yoghurt or ice cream tub. Add 1.5 cups of plaster of Paris, and stir gently with the stick to make a creamy mixture.

Paleontologists dig up fossils of ancient living things, millions of years after fossils form.

4.

Step 4.

With an adult to help, pour plaster of Paris into your moulds, filling them to the top. Leave them to set for at least an hour. Then carefully peel away the plasticine to reveal the fossil casts.

5.

Step 5.

Leave the casts for a few more hours to dry out completely. If you like, you can then paint them in greyish-brown colours to look like real stone.

MAGICAL CREATURES

To make a mysterious magical fossil, make a tiny mermaid, unicorn or dragon skeleton from clay. When it's set, use it to make a fossil cast.

GLOSSARY

algae A group of plant-like living things that includes pond slime and seaweeds.

animation Using a sequence of still images to create an illusion of life and movement.

anthocyanin A red, purple or blue chemical found in some plants.

bacteria A type of tiny living thing that can be seen using a microscope.

biology The study of life and living things.

breeding To select particular living things and encourage them to reproduce or have babies, in order to develop particular features.

carbon dioxide A gas that is produced by some types of living things.

cells The small units that living things are made up of.

chlorophyll A green chemical found in plants, used to help them make food using energy from sunlight.

condense To change from a gas into a liquid.

DNA (short for deoxyribonucleic acid) The spiral-ladder-shaped, string-like chemical that genes are made from.

double helix A shape similar to a ladder twisted into a spiral.

ecosystem A habitat and the living things in it, working together as a system.

entomologist A scientist who studies insects.

evaporate To change from a liquid into a gas.

fossil The shape or imprint of something that was once alive, preserved in rock.

fungi A group of living things that includes mushrooms, moulds and yeast.

genes Sections of DNA containing instructions that tell cells what to do, and control how a living thing grows and works.

instinct An automatic behaviour in an animal, which it does not have to learn.

lens A curved, transparent object used to make light bend, or refract, as it passes through it.

life cycle The series of changes a living thing goes through as it is born, grows up and has its own young.

minerals Pure, non-living substances found in nature, such as iron or quartz.

molecule A tiny single unit of a substance, made from even smaller units called atoms.

oxygen A gas found in the air, which animals need to breathe in order to survive.

palaeontologist A scientist who studies fossils and the history of life on Earth.

pigment A natural colouring chemical, especially one found in a living thing.

pupa An insect in the stage of development between a larva and an adult insect.

sound waves Waves made up of molecules vibrating to and fro, which spread out through the air or another substance as sound travels through it.

species The scientific name for a particular type of living thing.

terrarium A transparent, enclosed container for keeping plants or other living things alive inside.

translucent Letting light through, but blurring it so that objects are not clearly visible.

water cycle The sequence of stages water goes through as it moves between the sky, the sea and the land.

FURTHER INFORMATION

WEBSITES

Science Kids: Biology
www.sciencekids.co.nz/biology.html

Education.com: Life Science Activities and Experiments
www.education.com/activity/life-science/

BBC Bitesize: Fossils
www.bbc.co.uk/bitesize/articles/z22g7p3

WEBSITES ABOUT MAKING

Tate Kids: Make
www.tate.org.uk/kids/make

PBS Design Squad Global
pbskids.org/designsquad

Instructables
www.instructables.com

Make:
makezine.com

WHERE TO BUY MATERIALS

Hobbycraft
For art and craft materials
www.hobbycraft.co.uk

B&Q
For pipes, tubing, wood, glue and other hardware
www.diy.com

Fred Aldous
For art and craft materials,
photography supplies and books
www.fredaldous.co.uk

BOOKS

BOOM! Science: Living Things by Georgia
Amson-Bradshaw (Wayland, 2018)

Science in a Flash: Living Things by Georgia
Amson-Bradshaw (Franklin Watts, 2017)

Explanatorium of Nature
(Dorling Kindersley, 2017)

Living Things (Science in Infographics)
by Jon Richards (Wayland, 2017)

PLACES TO VISIT

Science Museum, London, UK
www.sciencemuseum.org.uk

Natural History Museum, London, UK
www.nhm.ac.uk/

The Ashmolean, Oxford UK
www.ashmolean.org/

Chicago Field Museum, Chicago, USA
www.fieldmuseum.org/

INDEX